Poems from Nowhere

Lewis Chandler

Contents.

Short.

Poems needn't have any rules. Sometimes even the shortest of verses can tap into the deepest of emotions.

Fear.

I detest your pain;
I fear its unblinking confidence,
As it stares me down,
Reveling in its own power,
And threatens to consume me too.

Lost.

Through the gap in time, they come,
Glimpses of lives now unknown,
For a brief second I'm there within,
Myself and more in another home.
Like a lost soul, I yearn to feel,
Those that guide me to a safe place,
But the way they rise, the same they fall,
And thus leave me cold, without a trace.

Dissolve.

Once he discovered he had nothing to prove,
He dissolved into stillness and spoke no more.

Peripheral Sanity.

My eye, blind to reality,
Conspires with my mind,
To try and preach insanity,
Lights flicker and burn,
A dreamscape in return,
Blurring and blending lines,
In a life bereft of clarity.

Incentives.

Desire for synchronicity,
Similarly, simplicity,
Burn your heart out quick,
You don't need one in this city,
Keep those features looking pretty;
That's your carrot and your stick.

Shine.

And the heavens spiraled downwards to the abyss below,
Consuming all darkness that presumed to feast on
existence,
The light of freedom shone effortlessly through the chains
of fear,
Illuminating that which was false and unknowingly
destructive.

Pray.

These poems are prayers,
Cast out upon the sky,
A burning passion,
Deep and true and mine.

Baggage.

I landed in front of you,
Stripped down and alone,
You picked up my baggage,
And you gave me a home.

Weeds.

Freedom of creation,
Explodes once I leave,
There is no inspiration,
To be found amongst the weeds.

Finite.

Don't mistake the finite world of thoughts,
For the total sum of your being;
Your light far outshines the words in your head.

Cosmos.

I could not tell of beauty,
With the words I was given, young,
So I vowed to search the cosmos,
For a way it could be done.

Discovery.

Mysterious discoveries,
Unique yet universal,
A personal recovery,
And an egoic reversal.

Fourteen.

Fourteen times you called my name,
Fourteen times I felt the same,
An old and dusty picture frame,
The distant dregs of what we became.

The Chase.

She knew that chasing sunsets would bear her no fruit,
But the promise of adventure kept her feet dancing in the
dusk.

Smile.

Our first act of defiance,
Was to smile wide;
There would be no more compliance,
There'd be no more to hide.

Undercover Living.

I think I dreamed this life before,
Deep down I know what's behind the door,
The careful reveal of each surprise,
Is a former lifetime deep in disguise.

Solarity.

The sun offered me its advice,
To me in hushed tones,
Carefully outlining its plans,
Of gold and one of bones.

Crazy Talk.

You may say I'm crazy,

but the voices in my head conspired to save me.

Re-run.

My dreams keep replaying,
Forgotten ones, re-run,
The scenes keep me praying,
That this freedom's just begun.

Definitions.

Imagine if your beauty.
Was not defined by others,
But by you,
And your loving heart.

AM.

I want art and music to crash like cymbals above my head;
At the same time, to whisper lovingly, by my side as I sink
into dreams;
To follow my heart to its last beat; to sing my legacy as
angels will;
To accompany me with snow or fire;
And keep others warm, as they do for me so readily upon
each breath.

Clouds.

The dancing clouds looked
down upon
our heads
and sang of the joys we created.
Together we conquered,
the universe.

Again.

So often déjà vu hooks me,
With a vibrant certainty,
Time slows down as fate washes over.
Engulfing me for just a few,
But overwhelmingly sure, seconds.

Dreams.

My soul dreams of places my body could never reach,
An undiscovered nirvana where only I dwell,
Alone but not lonely,
With the faint hum of life around me.

Reboot.

A midsize chunk of vital source,
The consumption of which realigned my course,
The strengthening of a once known power,
To face the demons from which I oft cower.

W1.

Slow down wild one,
Your heart will last a while,
There's no need to guard your love,
Or hide your broken smile.

Done&Dusted.

Capacity for brilliance,
Hamstrung.
Resolve and resilience,
Undone.

Riches Anew.

Broad-backed idealist,
Upon horse, high; realist,
Out of time; fearless.

Screens.

Fuck these screens,
Of endless scenes;
No depth.

The way it dries,
My big blue eyes;
I wept.

Seasonal Distaste.

Winter failed us,
But revolutions only succeed,
When former foundations fail.

The approach we take to Spring,
Reflects our character,
And shines our souls through to Summer.

Contrast.

Dark clouds,
Thick fog,
A noisy storm.

Sunshine,
Clear views,
Now I feel warm.

Store-room Survival.

Vacant space,
Behind a friendly face,
Artificial colour,
In an empty place.

Abject boredom,
Maintaining decorum,
Sitting pretty,
In a soulless store-room.

Faithful.

I crave a quick fix,
Comfort in pill form.
A touch from a stranger,
To leave my bed warm.

Be my rescue,
Set me up for good,
Faithful in kind,
Like this boy once could.

Swing.

The pendulum,
The seasons,
Passers-by,
No reasons.

Below in my chamber,
I can't see the sun,
But aloft like a kite,
I'm the only one.

Leap.

My life's poetry,
Leapt to its demise,
And bled.

It faked its death,
And wore a disguise,
Instead.

Mars.

Abstract thoughts,
Of the life we bought,
On Mars.

I was caught,
On words, distraught,
And stars.

Haikus.

Five-Seven-Five. I find haikus can be incredibly expressive with just seventeen syllables.

2-to-go.

Two minutes to go,
Midnight fast approaches us,
Alas we sit still.

Glass.

Unclean reflection,
Your body negates the heat,
Inside your glass cell.

Disquiet.

Eerie, broken place,
Silence underneath it all;
Wrong side of the tracks.

Home.

There is a peace in,
Domesticated living,
Under this shelter.

Peace.

In that Holy Place,
With silence and space abound,
I sought my refuge.

Voice.

Hold that anger there,
Inside with your beating heart,
Listen to its words.

Expansion.

I was one, then two,
Now three; but ten thousand things,
Reside within me.

Love.

A small collection of poems influenced by love.

Chasm.

The sort of person that inspires art and music,
In a vain attempt to replicate the beauty within her,
A tragic circumstance for those who would chance to love
her,
Only to realise she can never be theirs; for she is not even
her own,
Solemnly I guard the place in my heart where her voice
sings,
Echoing lustfully 'round the chasm where future lovers will
stake their claim,
Like a fool I fell for her, reckless and suicidal,
Yet I would tumble into that oblivion a thousand times
and more.

Waves.

I was there once,
Standing before the crashing waves.
They threatened to demolish it all,
But you were there beside me.

Obstacles.

An obstacle twice removed,
A fork in the road,
But I took both paths,
Just to get to you.

Starlight.

The stars went out,
But your light never did,
It shone bright enough,
For all the suns,
That had been exhausted,
By infinity.

Together.

There are moments of vulnerability that lovers share,
Ones that are only accessible to those that become part of
us,
These are the times we can truly take off the mask,
To stop pretending we are not scared.

Timeless.

I am rarely required,
To engage my brain,
When I'm with you,
That is to say-
It is pure,
Timeless,
Existence.

Tonic.

Her soul was white,
Pure like ice and untouched snow,
Her past though was deep and dark,
Cavernous and all-consuming,
And it was here she made her home,
Unaware of her own true essence,
Clinging effortlessly to her frame.

He came striding knowingly into her path,
And the life he brought with him was like a tonic to her
woes,
And even her once-shadowed smiles,
Became vibrant and wondrous.

Political.

We live in an ever-increasingly diverse political sphere. Here are some words found inside when pondering the state of the world.

Receipts.

The day we killed the sunset.
We jumped up out 'our seats,
And searched our dying world,
For we hoped we'd kept receipts.

Data Direction.

Data is the new currency,
Of a world inherently misguided,
A directionless computer,
With a battleground inside it.

Mutual.

I am constantly bemused,
By those who truly believe,
That men's and women's rights,
Are mutually exclusive.

Run&Pray.

Do you remember the day we left the world,
To burn and rot and then decay?
Do you recall how we used it all,
Then tripped and stumbled and ran away?
We flew too close to the sun somehow,
We knew we chose our guns and now,
There's nothing left to rest our bones,
The burnt lakes fight to ingest our homes.

Halos.

You cover yourselves in purchased glories,
Adorn your shriveled souls with dirty gold,
Crushed and bent into shape by the dust of skeletons,
The velvet of your best garments stained with blood,
From afar you may appear as Angels,
Designer diamonds sparkle above heads,
Alas, whatever your black heart touches turns to dust;
Halos aren't going to save you.

See-through.

Although transparency is a trait you seldom have,
We see through your well-worn games,
And your soul has faded to but a shimmer,
It manifests itself within your cold art,
And the plastic beach you present,
All the while grinning from the invisible chords in the
corner of your mouth,
Sitting upon the ventriloquist's lap,
A shimmering mirage of sweat pours down your face,
Distorting the lines of your made up visage,
Anxiously acting out the script you still somehow believe
will fool us,
Your authenticity sacrificed for cheap tricks and expensive
illusions,
The irony being we would all prefer honesty and humility,
And your inability to grasp that minimises your worth,
Making you ineffectual and evermore impotent with each
passing lie.

Listen&Learn.

Our gods are lost,
And prophets muted,
We aimlessly stray,
Sedated by instant pleasure.
We became binary people,
Who default to the comfort of mobile phones,
Ignorantly assuming we know best,
And that life will bend to our will,
We mistook our infinite potential,
For our fledgling ability,
A teenage society,
Believing our own words above others,
Pushing our limits beyond reason,
And screaming at the sky in angst,
We struggle for meaning,
Directionless and impatient,
If only we were grateful,
For the riches provided,
And listened once in a while,
To the wisdom in our hearts.

Snap.

Screenshots and snapchats and soundbites;
We are reducing our lives down to single frames,
Almost as in attempting to freeze a part of history,
Solidifying it along with our form,
Parts of us stuck forever in time,
As though they represent us more than our infinite essence
burning inside,
And extrapolating each other's character from one tiny
morsel of information,
Taking one airbrushed sentence and attacking,
Chasing others out of town and expelling them from the
crowd,
Removing their rights with forceful anger,
At the one slip away from moral virtue,
Or for offering an alternative opinion to our apparently
truthful own,
One that doesn't tally up with our freeze-frame, our
smiling avatar,
The shallows that shimmer, disguised as deep pools,
For our judgements are borrowed and our thoughts are on
loan,
All a maximum of ten seconds long, of course, so attention
never fades.

Strings.

The puppets have left the circus,
To practice their pageantry,
Their livelihood at stake,
In the opinions of you and me.

They've buffed their wooden hearts,
And glossed their pompous smiles,
Set their affairs in order,
And destroyed those hidden files.

Once again they strut around,
Fuelled by a monst'rous diet,
Of shouting out their egos loud,
And keeping their mistresses quiet.

But their golden hours can't last forever,
There's transience in all things,
We'll stop listening to their heinous lies.
And indignantly cut their strings.

Mental.

These poems document my struggles with depression, anxiety and general mental-health issues.

Romancing the Bones.

It's quite romantic,
To be depressed,
In a world so giving,
A personal Hell,
In the land of the living,
Unshakable intimacy with the dark,
Death mixed with your essence,
Fire whimpers and ice melts,
Flowers wilt and skies grey,
Oh!
If only,
That was it,
Without,
The searing heat of anger,
Crashing into your tired bones,
The deafening loneliness,
The incessant depressant,
Screaming in your head,
The iron knots that tie you to your bed,
Twisting, binding,
Tearing, scratching,
Eating away at your energy,

Like carrion crows with a blood lust,
Harsh winds blow in every direction,
And without your hardened skin for protection,
Your heart cannot beat in rhythm with your loved ones,
And your mind spends its time fighting shadows,
All the while the demons screech louder,
All the while you're stranded in the wilderness,
But no search party comes because no-one knows you're lost,
Your scars are invisible so others don't notice when they rip them open,
You implode and explode simultaneously,
And the pieces don't exactly fit back together the way you remember,
Your reflection grimaces back at you,
Unrecognisable man in the mirror,
You try to smile back but you find you're no longer in control,
Of the bones you once believed you owned.

Bleed.

Chasing peace through the fog of uncertainty,
Left me naked and crippled,
And my heart raw,
From the ongoing attempts to set it alight.

Constant.

Pressure might create diamond,
But a man can fail to shine as bright,
Losing consciousness swiftly and sadly,
The light fading into but a faint glow,
The closing of doors and hearts and minds;
Fires from frying pans is no means of escape,
Thus agreements are entered into with demons,
While awaiting rescue from the depths.

Community.

The best times seldom come,
On one's own, without company,
It is in communion with others,
That our hearts sing and souls roar,
Coming together with people,
Be it friends, family, strangers,
Brings us closer to ultimate truth,
And lights the path to salvation.

Progression.

This staunch denial of self,
The anxious teen from your past,
Attempting to escape the perils of reality,
Running scared is antithetical behaviour,
To your commitment of growth,
You will prosper greatly,
If only you are prepared to let it die.

Piercing.

Bound by rules,
And trapped in confined spaces,
The jagged words beneath my skin-
That run like lava through the cracked dirt left by the
stories before them-
Pierce my lungs,
And scorch my eardrums with ember,
They tear away my eyelids,
Their talons scratch at my skull.

Endless, endless.
Darkness, darkness.

Fall.

Expressions

Falling

Fast-

No light in the room,
For a boy and his addictions –

Thoughts cracked and bent,
Lie broken,
And his feelings have fled –

He left them no choice,
When he filled the space with glass,
Shards of opportunity smashed in the void-

And a forgotten memory laid upon the doorstep, covered
in grime.

Cement.

Ready to scream,
But my words are cement,
They sit idly by,
But armed with intent.

Fadeaway.

If bound by others' insistence,
Do you truly exist?
Your imprint on the world dissolves,
And is replaced by a shadow,
An avatar at the behest of them-
They, whom you made your God-
A wind-up doll walking circles,
Soul captured and wasted,
As you retreat from the world,
Monotonous and plain and inoffensive,
All remnants of character ground down,
Leaving but a smiling cardboard cut-out.

Screech.

Let life cut me,
Burn my heart,
Leave scars across my chest,
Rip apart my body,
Let it punch me in the gut,
Throw me to the wolves,
Drop me in the ocean,
And wipe me clean from the Earth.

Let me feel all these things deep within me,
For then I would know I have lived.

Passenger.

What propels this vehicle along,
Makes its decisions,
Ignites its engine?
I watch the road move through fogged-up passenger-side window,
Attempting, oft with futility,
To make sense of the scenery before me,
White knuckled and with chewed fingertips,
Anxiously searching for signposts,
And inwardly pleading for deceleration,
Somewhere just out of reach is a spark of an idea,
Of commandeering the ship,
Along with far off memories of me as pilot.

Shadowspace.

Wanting to hide,
But I'm still in plain sight,
There's a pain my side,
And this day is too bright.

Grief stretches wide,
As I withdraw from the fight,
My words have all lied,
I am disguised from the light.

Reignite.

Poetry and I fell out of love with each other,
When I forgot how to love,
I became shallow and disinterested,
As well as uninteresting,
The content of my conversations,
Were dull, and spent,
The light behind my eyes left for a better gig,
And not for reasons I'd held,
My strength borrowed from the bottle,
Stories intertwined with dampened reasoning,
This pony's only trick,
Concerned with style over substance,
I now understand that when I fall out of love,
I fall hard,
Out of love with life and its quirks,
But that despite the rain,
The flame can be reborn.

Anchor.

Anchored by anxiety,
And the way my brain would lie to me,
It was the dark night of my soul,
That had stolen my sobriety.

Cell.

The lack of silence has exhausted me,
And encased my brain in dust,
My prison's walls echo with insanity,
Captured my someone's else's imagination.

Diagnosis.

It's not anxiety,
Forget ADHD too,
It's A-D-W-D,
For "Any Distraction Will Do".

Voice.

Whose voice is that...
That paces 'round my head,
Putting the world to rights,
Finding fault in others,
While clouding up my inner space?

His views are most unwelcome!

Worn.

Thoughts, persistent,
Should meet resistance,
But my barriers were worn.

The deadly night,
Put up a fight,
And left my heart forlorn.

Ocean Wisdom.

A seasoned sailor I may be,
Hard from harsh weather and with wisdom abound,
But these thunderous waves have captured my sanity,
And taken my good sense hostage.

Lunar-Sea.

Strange the way,
The tide came back in.

I thought the moon had given up,
On its partnership with the waves.

Spiritual.

Many answers to this complicated universe can be found within. These poems look inwards in an attempt to answer burning questions about existence.

Who Am I?

Within me,
There is
A poet;
A cynic;
A monk;
A fighter;
A child;
A monster.

And always
The question
Who Am I?

Soulsearch.

There is no map that points to the soul,
Descriptive words lack substance,
A multitude of directions arise,
There is but one that guides you.

Dust.

We cling to happiness,
With vice-like grip,
For reassurance that the world loves us.

But we squeeze too tight,
Suffocate its nature,
And it diminishes and dwindles to dust.

We must let it go,
Like the passing clouds,
And trust it will return to show its affection once more.

Emptiness.

Emptiness could not hold itself back from the precipice;
It yearned to break through and be realised.

Source.

Electric,
Clear;
an immovable force.

Eccentric,
Dear;
the inconceivable Source.

Alarm Clock.

How can I be two?
One, feverishly fearful,
A voice of angst and longing,
So angry and timid.

Set against the purest peace,
An ever-present presence,
Unmoved by the internal muttering,
And external battles

The truth is, I cannot be both,
It becomes clear which I am,
Yet this fact is troubling,
Reality has been but an illusion.

Here.

Future's hand reaching,
Into now's domain,
But part of the teaching,
Is to just remain,
Stay centred here,
Resist the temptations,
To succumb to fear,
And maintain your patience.

Awareness.

Look closely,
At the element of existence,
That is ever present.

Your face may age,
The seasons will cycle,
Your thoughts arise and fall.

But notice the continuing presence,
In the background of all of this;
You are aware.

Observe.

If you watch,
With no judgement,
You begin to align.

Fight.

Peace is ever-present,
It resides in silence,
And the space between your thoughts,
All has its own grace,
So don't fight the waves,
The tide will always return to the shore.

Illumination.

Clouds may form, deep, dense,
Obscuring your vision,
Yet the sky is never harmed,
It loses nothing of its essence.

You are the sky, infinite, vast,
The clouds: your thoughts and feelings,
They pass through you and disappear,
You lose nothing of your essence.

It may appear the weather is your true form,
It seems its composition is you,
But the ever-unchanging limitlessness of the sky,
Is the impossible nothingness of your essence.

Calm.

Align in harmony,
With all and the rest,
Silence within you,
Will empty you of sin.

You.

You are no fixed point,
Time does not pivot around you,
You are fluid, ever-changing,
Constantly flowing with everything.

Long.

Long-form poems can tell more of the story. This collection is in various styles, covering numerous topics.

Future Imperfect.

What of poetry, then?
What of its soulful telling of pain, when our upgraded
bodies no longer remember what that feels like?
Or what love, horror, sex and pride taste like;
What of that awful yearning, of despair of not achieving.
Of glorious sunshine breaking through windows on a
spring morning?
What of all this when we have everything we want, all at a
click,
Of fingers or of buttons, and of any possibility?
What will these be, when our dreams are planted directly
into our minds and reality becomes merged with unreality?
What is pure when all exists artificially and in abundance?
What are we when we no longer choose to feel, all of it,
any of it?
What is life when we hide it away in boxes and sweep it
under rugs;
When we polish our bodies, as we do fruit, so that only sex
and lust exist?
What, therefore, is the sense in pursuing scientific
breakthrough without a cause greater than aesthetics and
soulless, pornographic nothingness?

Beauty in Defeat.

I aimed high but ultimately could not reach the precipice,
The summit I yearned for eluded me,
The riches I sought were not easily obtained,
On the mountain so treach'rous of terrain.

For twas not my battle to overcome,
I fell victim to murd'rous forces within,
Each told a story of the deepest darkness,
Their powers drawn from demons of old.

Yet this is no warning to future heroes,
Who might attempt the feat as I did,
I may have been defeated in my task,
But the beauty of the mountain was the treasure I gained.

Acid Grey.

It sits beneath the lines,
Interrupted in its flow,
Outlet needs refining,
The cylinders realigning,
The clouds need a new lining,
Silver too far gone now,
So this needs redefining,
A deeper grey,
Is more what we know,
If we insist on clouds at all,
The acid rain needs a home,
Aloft, to threaten us with our own survival.

The Raven.

The winter tide obscured the raven's vision,
Covered its wings in dust,
Singing dutifully, it ignored the obstacles ahead,
And made for the shelter of the old oak tree.

Cradled in its nest, aloft in the weathered branches,
It scanned its surroundings,
What once was a dense and luscious forest,
Had been squandered and reduced to waste.

The raven held its own, private reservations,
On the topic at hand;
The people could not be blamed for their folly,
How were they to know how unforgiving nature could be?

Man had detached himself from the other creatures,
Had become like stone,
Lifeless and careless without thought for the Earth,
And had turned it to ash, and died in the rubble.

Uninhibited.

Love, inhibited,
Became a stow-away in another's vision,
And hidden by ghosts,
That were conjured by ancestors,
Of spirit, not of blood,
Although much of that was readily spilt,
In a need for truth to out,
Dragging it into the open with all might expended,
Combusting in the heat of hate,
Spotlight burning brands onto faces of the doomed,
Proudly consumed and crippled by all of it,
Spinning in time to the flow of a cosmos,
Inhabited by love.

Empires.

Damaged goods, saving face,
Empires of the human race,
Hid down in our darkened eyes,
Lives our treasure chest of lies,
Broken arrows falling fast,
This next verse might be our last,
We bravely smile at Fate's cruel stare,
The silent truth of our despair.

The Foolish King.

Left untethered,
The usurper climbs,
Holds the seat of power captive,
Tightens its grip,
Blocks the sun from view,
Erodes the progress made before.

Resurgence comes from lack of discipline,
Focus otherwise spent,
Burning up resources,
Taking all for granted,
Immature wanting after lust,
Power distracts the foolish King.

The polished mirror however,
Strengthens the resistance,
Keeps those that would revolt in check,
Quells the urge for chaos,
The seas become calm,
And the armies remain at attention.

The fool becomes the wise,
His presence ushers in the new dawn,
Scars begin to heal with natural remedies,
The shadow across the land retreats,
The golden light shines eternal,
And peace reigns with joy.

On Bermondsey St.

On Bermondsey Street,
One of the first beautifully sunny days of the year,
Further highlighting the area's similarity to a seaside town,
Of small, colourful shops and of warehouses.

On a crowded green,
Hundreds of people escaping the tyranny of office air
conditioning,
Impromptu picnics and cigarettes and removed cardigans,
And all-too ambitious locals seeking a summer.

Writing this, a cynic,
Who came here to find refuge from the almost identical
crowds,
In a cramped office with suffocating artificial air released
from vents,
An attempt to get away from screens and screaming
boredom.

Ironic it is,
That this was written on a mobile phone,
With notebook forgotten,
Furthermore, the location: in the shade, soggy grass-
and also without company,
And the realisation that the funny smell comes from
nearby refuse truck.

Three men walk past,
All in black,
Juxtaposition for the others in vests.

Garbageman throws sack full of rubbish,
It misses the truck and lands on the floor,
Offending the scene, which attempted to be lovely.

Perhaps the case,
Really is the company, which the cynic finds himself
without,
Yearning for the chatter that those around him have in
abundance,
On Bermondsey Street, on a crowded green.

Index.

Printed in Great Britain
by Amazon